Hajer Alriyami was born in Abu Dhabi, in 1991. She graduated from the Higher College of Technology in business quality and strategic management in 2016. She completed her master of business administration at Abu Dhabi University by the year 2021. She is now pursuing higher education DBA program at Abu Dhabi University. Ms. Hajer Alriyami is an administrative officer who joined Zayed University in 2018. Hajer believes that volunteering and helping others bring joy and fulfillment to her life and the lives of others.

I dedicate this book to my family and friends.

Hajer Alriyami

My Journey Through the Essentials and Quality of Education

AUSTIN MACAULEY PUBLISHERS™
LONDON • CAMBRIDGE • NEW YORK • SHARJAH

Copyright © Hajer Alriyami 2023

The right of Hajer Alriyami to be identified as author of this work has been asserted by the author in accordance with Federal Law No. (7) of UAE, Year 2002, Concerning Copyrights and Neighboring Rights.

All rights reserved. No part of this publication may be reproduced, stored in a retrieval system, or transmitted in any form or by any means, electronic, mechanical, photocopying, recording, or otherwise, without the prior permission of the publishers.

Any person who commits any unauthorized act in relation to this publication may be liable to legal prosecution and civil claims for damages.

The age group that matches the content of the books has been classified according to the age classification system issued by the Ministry of Culture and Youth.

ISBN – 9789948792796 – (Paperback)
ISBN – 9789948792802 – (E-Book)

Application Number: MC-10-01-9599800
Age Classification: E

Printer Name: iPrint Global Ltd
Printer Address: Witchford, England

First Published 2023
AUSTIN MACAULEY PUBLISHERS FZE
Sharjah Publishing City
P.O Box [519201]
Sharjah, UAE
www.austinmacauley.ae
+971 655 95 202

First and foremost, thanks to the God, the Almighty, for His showers of blessings throughout my journey in education and life, and for helping me complete this book successfully.

There are many people I would like to express my thanks to. I will start by expressing my deep and sincere gratitude to my family for all their prayers and support. Without them, I would not be here today and complete this achievement.

I would like to thank the universities (HCT, ADU, and ZU) that supported me by giving me the best knowledge and creating opportunities to meet great people who encouraged me.

My gratitude and deepest appreciation to the only person who supported me academically and walked with me step by step through my academic journey: Ms. Catherine Journeaux. I believe that without her I wouldn't have been able to complete my MBA.

My sincere thanks and appreciation to Dr. Nadine Jaafarawi and Dr. Ileana Baird who, despite being very busy, stood by me and supported me in writing this book.

My gratitude and deepest appreciation to my best friends and colleagues. Every one of you have something unique and taught me something valuable, thank you for standing by my side and making my journey memorable and enjoyable. Thanks for all your support and good wishes. I wish you all the best in all aspects of your life.

My appreciation goes to the contributors Dr. Areej, Dr. Efthymia, and Dr. Nadine. Thank you for your support and for making the accomplishment achieved. Each one has added her specialty to my book.

Finally, my appreciation goes to the publisher, auditor, and all the people who have encouraged me to complete this book, either directly or indirectly.

Table of Contents

Contributors	**11**
Introduction	**14**
Section One	**16**
Essentials of Education	*20*
The Importance of Education in the UAE	*28*
Set a Plan for Future and Career	*34*
Time Management	*41*
Health and Education	*49*
Why I Need a Higher Qualification?	*60*
Final Thoughts	*64*
Section Two: My Educational Journey	**68**
Before Joining the School	*71*
Primary School	*75*
What Happened Next?	*78*
Where the Challenges Started	*81*

The Most Frightening Experience Happened in My Life	*84*
To the Last Step Before My Next Journey	*88*
Summary of Advice	**92**
Bibliography	**97**

Contributors

Dr. Areej Elsayary

Dr. Areej ElSayary joined the College of Education at Zayed University as an Assistant Professor. She has 11 years' experience, with specific expertise in Science, Technology, Engineering, Art, and Mathematics (STEAM), curriculum design and development, teaching and learning, assessment, and schools accreditation. Prior to joining Zayed University, she was working at the Al Arabia for Education Company, as well as being Adjunct Faculty at the American University and inspecting schools. She is an Approved Accreditation Visitor from New England Association of School and Colleges (NEASC) and Council of International School (CIS). Her research interests include the cognitive development, Interdisciplinary STE(A)M curriculum, and assessment. She has published her work internationally and has presented papers at conferences. Dr. Areej has also conducted several teacher trainings including the MOE Arab Teacher Gulf Forum. She is currently involved in research and creative projects. She has an active research agenda and collaborates internationally on creative research projects.

Dr. Efthymia Efthymiou

Dr. Effie Efthymiou has extensive experience in designing and conducting qualitative methods research in inclusive and special education. Her research interests pertain to inclusion, and educational environments, which are conducive to supporting inclusive class teaching from the point of view of stakeholders, particularly children with SEND and how far the physical as well as psychological environments contribute to positioning and attitudes. She has served as principal and co-investigator on numerous research grants that have focused on enhancing the quality of teaching and schooling for special populations. She is the author or co-author of peer-reviewed journal articles on issues pertaining to the education and inclusion of students with mild/moderate disabilities from a multimodal research perspective.

Dr. Nadine Jaafarawi

Nadine Jaafarawi is a PhD holder in Applied Linguistics. She is a researcher and has several publications in the field of Applied Linguistics and Early Childhood Education. She has presented in several conferences, locally and internationally. Her teaching profile extends to more than 20 years. She was a preschool teacher, English coordinator, and curriculum developer in Lebanon for more than 15 years. She was a lecturer at the Lebanese University, Lebanese International University, and Saint Joseph University for more than six years. She joined Zayed University, an assistant professor, in spring 2018. A dynamic work environment with amazing opportunities to deploy the latest and greatest in education and technology. She is a 'fellow' in the Higher Education Academy (Advance HE), and a member in the EmSAT National Committee for Grade 1 Baseline Assessment at the Ministry of Education in Abu Dhabi. In this year, she joined the membership of ALLT (applied linguistics and Language Teaching International Conference and Exhibition) and now the coordinator of the reading Groups initiated by ALLT. Her current research involves the development of teaching methodologies and approaches that will enhance students' literacy skills, bilingual development of early years' children in the gulf, parental intervention in early years, and online education issues.

Introduction

I hope you're one of the people who either stopped education for a long time or approaching graduation with a bachelor or a master's degree and need that push to continue the journey. So, get ready because I'm about to give this push. Before that, please note any stories ideas that came to your mind and share them with me at the end. Have you thought about how to be unique from others? Have you wondered why we need to finish university and why our parents are eagerly waiting for us to earn the degree? Education is a powerful tool that could distinguish you from others socially and at work. This book will present ideas that might change your mind about pursuing higher education.

The division of the book will reveal a list of topics where I discuss why education is essential for self-improvement by sharing my journey. This book is conversation book instead of reflected analyzed theriacal published therefore you find lack of reference. Celebration of your small steps in making your next life-changing judgment with best aspirations.

This book will be divided in two parts. The first part will be focused on the importance of education for myself and why I think people should pursue to higher education. This section will also cover the importance of education in the UAE, and the role of the leaders with examples. Moreover, this section will highlight the benefits of setting a short and long goal, plan for future and career, and how that could support individual's vision. Section one will explore time management from other significant. Lastly, this section will look at the relationship between health and education whether if it impacts individuals, performance particularly for people with health condition.

The second part of the book will be focused on my experience through my educational journey in school and university. Also, this section will illustrate stories that happened during my educational journey. I will share some of the advice to overcome the difficulty wishing that it benefits you. I hope that you will find this book valuable as you travel.

Section One

Education is a non-stop journey, and it depends on the individuals' goals and where they see themselves in their career or in the future. People always ask me how pursuing an MBA (Master of Business Administration) will benefit me and my answer is always that it is a part of my self-development. This is essential, particularly for a master's degree because everyone admires those who keep going forward and not those who have no dreams to chase, who remain in the same spot. Rather than being pessimistic, we should embrace the challenge and encourage each other to complete our education. However, to do so, we need to have a plan that takes us from one level to another. In other words, you need to plan out for what you want to be even if that takes time, it will be a rewarding achievement that will stay with you forever in your future career.

Education is the key element to people's success in life and career more than non-educated people like secure job and stability. Choosing the right major will help you incessantly in your professional journey. It is unfortunate that fresh high school graduates see a university degree as a thing that needs to be obtained and then move on. This may be because of the lack of awareness from society and the teachers in schools. It is imperative to be aware of the importance of choosing the right major so that students really use their creativity to succeed. Also, students should know that there is no shame or waste of time in changing your major, particularly in their first year in a major.

As an example of choosing the major, I remember choosing between health and business as I was interested and still in both. I thought about it, and several reasons stopped me from selecting a health major personally; it might be different for you. Firstly, physically I can't (you would know more in my educational journey section) as commonly people in the health sector tend to work for a long hour. The second reason working in the health sector, whether staff or in the medical crew, is a sensitive job working for vulnerable people. Every step is critical dealing with the patient's record in providing the most updated accurate data. Therefore, I decided to choose something I still love, and see myself in it. I further decided to look at health in my free time, like watching medical dramas, reading a book, speaking, and gathering with my friends from the college of health. Once again, this is my opinion of selecting a health major. If you are a health student, that is an incredible choice, and I assure you would make a difference in your society. The point here is whatever major you choose as long it brings joy to you and contributes the most to your life.

One more comment regarding the majors before moving to the reasons for completing higher education. You will come across people who discourage you when they hear your decision directly or indirectly. Keep ignoring them; it doesn't matter either your major was known, unknown, demanding, or the market sufficient from it. Be sure that the universities in the UAE won't open a major and let you study for x number of years if the market is adequate. Ministry of Education (Commission for Academic Accreditation department) extract an annual report presents these numbers and notify the colleges at university number of majors should be close and stay open.

There are several reasons why people stop before completing their education. The first reason and the most important one is program requirement: this is what almost prevented me from completing my education. Examples of the program requirement include GPA, Math test, English test, and other tests, depending on major (Art, IT, communication, business, etc.) and the program (bachelor, master, PhD). I will address this in more details in the next chapter educational journey. Another reason is unemployment, or delay in starting your career because many programs require experience. It takes time for a person to gain the experience, and, by that time, he or she may lose knowledge to pursue higher education. In addition, unemployment prevents you from paying the university fees; this is the third reason why people stop before completing their education. Lastly, the most common reason is shortage of time where the majority is working full time job and parenting at the same time. Regardless the reasons that could prevent people of completing high education. Furthermore, what needed here is two things work out slightly the barriers one by one and time management skill which I will explain later in the 'time management' section.

"Work to become, not to acquire."
— Elbert Hubbard

Essentials of Education

It would be an understatement to say that education is critical. Education is a weapon for bettering one's life that provides better conversation and better options in terms of workplace, position, and salary. It is probably the most effective way to change one's life; education unquestionably influences a person's life quality. Without one, you can't move, and even without higher education, you may not have the ability to move forward because of market changes and demand. Education broadens one's awareness and abilities while also shaping one's personality and attitude as it drives learners to think deeper and more comprehensively.

Most importantly, education is essential in improving people's chances of finding work. A simplistic example, you may compare students the first year and last year at the university, you will notice the level of knowledge enchantment is dramatically different. That applies to stopping education or not completing higher education, the level of knowledge from degree to higher level of degree is completely outstanding and pleasant.

The majority of us grow up learning about the importance of education for self-development. However, why is education important? During your grueling school or college years, you may have assumed it was a waste of time or just something you had to do to build a career. However, in reality, education reaches far beyond finding the best position and making your family happy. It is one of the most powerful weapons out there you can hold in your hands. Indeed, it journey tasks most of your time with challenges and stories as it gives work-life balance. Therefore, create a beautiful memory with your best friends and look for something that could make you happy, like volunteering to guide junior students or attending an activity, or working part-time at the university. These things would build a strong resume, personality as a leader, acculture your learning process, and minify the dependency on others.

So far, for sure, you have thought of your major and the choices you have to make, or you may have thought of the degree you completed and whether you want to pursue your higher education. Take some time now and think of what you want to be, and what you can do. By what you want to be I do not necessarily mean the typical answer, "I want to be a doctor," or "I want to be an engineer." What I meant is what major or degree could make you satisfied, feel like you are giving it your best and how, by this degree, you will best serve your beloved country.

There are unlimited and various reasons why education is important. One of the most important reasons is that education provides stability to an individual and supports building a family. Education grants security in life, and it is a thing that no one can take away from you. By getting a university degree, you boost your possibilities for more professional shots and open every day new doors for you. For instance, if your highest qualification is a bachelor's degree, if you to pursue a master's degree, you are more likely to get promoted or have a better job. For sure, most people would say that their jobs don't support higher qualification. However, your job is to seek for a better opportunity not only inside your work but also outside. I came to know people based in Ras Al-Khaimah who live here in Abu Dhabi because they found a better job that matches their qualifications. Another example is that many people move to the UAE for better job opportunities. With that being said, the key point is to be patient and keep trying every day to look for better opportunities.

The former reason supports the following reason: education gives you security in regard to your financial growth and income. An article written by Annie Mueller who is specializing in business and productivity called 'Education vs. Experience: Which One Gets the Job?' updated on 16 Dec 2020 explains that 'holding a degree or many on your resumes can provide job applicants an advantage in getting selected in the first place…' For instance, a 2018 report from the Association of American Colleges and Universities (AACU) discovered that 82% of executives and 75% of chosen managers surveyed think that it is essential for people today to complete a university education.

Moreover, according to Maslow's hierarchy of needs theory regarding the safety need, when an individual's physiological needs are relatively fulfilled and satisfied, their safety needs take preference and control behavior. In any absence of physical security due to war, natural disasters, or a lack of economic security, these security needs express themselves in various ways. These include the decision for professional safety, savings accounts, insurance policies, or accommodation. By far these are the strongest reasons and that's why the education gives stability to the people and not only secures their income but also enhances it.

Other reasons why people pursue higher education are developing skills such as problem-solving, decision-making, critical thinking, and negotiation in work and real life. Enhancing these skills could play a vital role in your present or future career. Self-improvement allows you to identify your potential and test yourself. Knowing your strengths is essential from a relationship and career perspective. It helps you better understand what you are looking for and where you can thrive and excel. According to Ramdass and Zimmerman, self-development is proactive in creating a solution rather than just reacting to it after things happened. They also added that being proactive means that 'individuals consistently organize and manage their thoughts, emotions, behaviors, and environment to attain academic goals.'

This applies to self-development as well: you protect yourself with a degree before someone asks you for one. For instance, you may find an opportunity that fits your experience and area; however, it requires a particular qualification which is higher than the one you completed. If your goal is to move to a higher position, you need to seek self-development. Self-development can raise self-awareness in the individual and overcome one's weaknesses. It also drives you to step out of your comfort zone as it did to me when I decided to start writing my book. It allows for healthier decision making in both career and life.

Furthermore, self-improvement could enhance your mental health as it motivates you and makes things more straightforward. Lastly, it can build self-love and make others (your line manager, co-workers, and family) proud of the accomplishments you're adding to your resume every day. On the other hand, self-development also could be beneficial and profitable for the company itself as its employees sharpen their existing skills. By providing them with a chance to shine, companies increase employee satisfaction and reduce employee turnover. That will lead to an increase in a business's performance and effectiveness.

The former reason supports the following reason: with given tools, knowledge, skills, financial security, and stability in life are achieved. This empowers one to make decisions and choose the right option in life: whether it is about admiration, a higher position, financial security, or family stability, education provides all of these and much more.

The final and most important reason why higher education is important is gaining confidence. Confidence is an essential feeling that leads individuals to perform and express themselves better. With confidence, your chance of reaching your goals is elevated. Completing your education can give you an incredible feeling of self-assurance, whether at work or in life. People can hear your confidence in your voice; that's why they say that, whenever you're presenting, what you say will sound true to others if you speak confidently.

Education is a spark of light in the dark. It is a promise for a better life. Education is the fundamental right of every person on this earth. Uneducated youth is the worst thing for humanity, as that could lead to an uncivilized society. Above all, it is the parents and governments' responsibility to ensure that education is given to everyone and disseminated.

By Dr. Nadine Jaafarawi
Envisioning Education

What is essential in education stems from the household. Parenting is an essential variable to offset the outcomes of a proper education. It is well-known that a school is a second home to students. Therefore, the proper foundation that prepares students for the world starts from their home. Later on, the objectives of teachers and educators will be rendered more achievable. From kindergarten to university, students need to be focused. Unfortunately, social media and electronic devices are a double-edged weapon to our generations. They can help students learn and at the same time, they tend to distract them. The objective of parents therefore is to limit the use of electronic devices to leaning purposes in order to create the proper foundation for educators.

Another essential aspect to education is shaping our world we live in today. Many educators inspire students to become engineers, teachers, nurses, doctors, etc....A curriculum that a school or university provides shapes the interest of students and molds them into what they want or aspire to become. Personally speaking, I have been teaching argumentation for a while and I believe this skill I am teaching students creates an objective perspective and open-mindedness they need to make informed decisions in their future careers. They question their opinion and the opinion of others to reach an objective stance at the end. Other educator who work with me also provide their input in order to arm students with adequate knowledge to guide them in their careers.

Skills, these elements are transferable by all means. Education is essential to diversify those skills and teach students the necessary survival techniques. Doctors, for example, need to be attentive to details in order to diagnose and find the right remedy for the patient. Another skill doctors should have is empathy, in order to practice adequate bedside manner. Even teachers of English as a second language have a role in helping students have a grasp of using this universal language in their daily lives.

Emotional intelligence is another skill a student needs to master. "Emotionally intelligent leaders can use their social skills to inspire and persuade this category of followers to adopt the proposed change and strive to contribute efficiently toward achieving the organizational goal." (Srivastava, 2013) With this being said, students are to be considered as potential leaders, mastering many skills including emotional intelligence. To define this skill and according to Srivastava (2013), emotional intelligence can best be defined as the capability to identify one's own and other people's emotions, to distinguish between different emotions and label them appropriately, and to use emotional information to guide thinking and behavior.

"The roots of education are bitter, but the fruit is sweet."
– Aristotle

The Importance of Education in the UAE

As per the UAE government portal, education is the constitutional right of every citizen. The United Arab Emirates government recognizes education's role in building a knowledge-based economy for the post-oil era. MoE (The Ministry of Education) has developed an Education 2020 strategy to create a world-class education system. The vision is to deliver a first-rate education that supports the National Agenda in line with this vision. One of the National Agenda's marks is that UAE students must be the best in the world in reading, mathematics, and science and have a deep knowledge of the Arabic language. The UAE government's higher education strategy 2030 is to offer future generations the needed technical and practical skills to lead the economy in public and private sectors. It also aims to prepare Emirati professionals who can maintain growth in vital sectors, such as knowledge, economy, entrepreneurship, and marketplace. Besides the Strategic Plan of the MoE, between 2017 and 2021, the goals are to assure a comprehensive quality of education, a culture of innovation, and a stimulating working atmosphere by keeping the students' interest as the highest priority.

Our leader H.H. Sheikh Mohamed bin Zayed Al Nahyan, the Crown Prince of Abu Dhabi and Deputy Supreme Commander of the UAE Armed Forces, Chairman of the Executive Council, and H.H. Mohammed bin Rashid Al Maktoum, the Vice President and Prime Minister of the United Arab Emirates and ruler of the Emirate of Dubai. They emphasized the role of education and support youth to complete education to be number one in distinct field like space sciences, and other fields. The following are examples of our leader's actions:

- Giving the ability and chance to other children inside and outside the UAE in underdeveloped nations to pursue their education so that they would have a way of living and increase their income. For example, as I mentioned earlier, the UAE government will build schools, send school stationery, games, and food, and provide textbooks, and learning materials to the existing schools. The following institutions have a hand in spreading education and knowledge:

  - Dubai Cares
  - Mohammed Bin Rashid Library
  - Mohammed Bin Rashid Al Maktoum Knowledge Foundation
  - School for 50 million Arabic students in cooperation with UNESCO, UNICEF and ISESCO
  - Arab Reading Challenge
  - The Knowledge Summit

- The Mohammed bin Rashid Al Maktoum Knowledge Award
- The Mohammed bin Rashid Arabic Language Award

- A great example is the action taken during the Covid-19 pandemic 2020. The UAE was the first country to quickly adopt distance learning. They bought the tools needed for all sectors, including the MoE, so that they could deliver courses and the students can get educated while they are stay safe at home (zoom, Microsoft team, WebEx, e-books, etc.).
- Recent news announcement moves are in line with His Highness Sheikh Mohammed bin Zayed Al Nahyan's directives to ensure that students continue their university education during the service period. The plan allows 12th-grade students of the 2020-2021 academic year to join the 16th batch and the subsequent batches and be enrolled in the university education through a 'distance learning' system. This move reflects the leadership's commitment to developing the national human workforce for the future and ensuring their entry into the national service while simultaneously continuing their university education smoothly and without interruption.
- As H.H. Mohammed bin Rashid Al Maktoum has emphasized, "The UAE is well aware of the importance of smart learning as it invested earlier in the digital infrastructure. Distance learning will be an integral part of the educational system…this is the

future." He created a digital school that will be launched by the end of year, September 2021. It will be the first alliance in the world focused on the future of digital education and he will support the implementation of the digital school across its various stages.
- By 2021, the UAE will have invested AED 386 million on innovation and entrepreneurship. 74,400 people will be the beneficiaries of innovation and entrepreneurship: 3,871 Emirati entrepreneurs will be supported by H.H Mohammed bin Rashied and 780,000 participants will be registered in the Million Arab Coders initiative.

Endless examples of actions took by our leaders in the UAE that need a designated book. Our leaders believe that bringing the best education to the UAE will secure the country's development. It will improve UAE's economy as more investors will be interested in our learning system. Not only will this initiative enhance the economy but also will give back to our community. As a person with business background, I would say that many expats in the UAE and the increase in the innovation by local and non-local small and medium entrepreneurs. That will drive UAE to become a leading country in the education sector and other sectors such as invitation, strategics, agriculture, business international, and sciences. That will also create a modern society that will provide the best knowledge through public, private, and online platforms.

By Dr. Nadine Jaafarawi

If the objectives of the UAE are to raise the academic ability of their students in order to reach internationally competitive levels and adapt to the diversity of a knowledge economy, education reform must be accompanied with a cultural shift. Furthermore, UAE policymakers can acquire from suggestions for advances from available research. For example, schools and teachers should be well-trained on discipline and integrity. Students should be trained to think critically using English *and* Arabic. Most importantly, cooperation between *all* stakeholders should be encouraged, having teachers' input included at every stage of the reform process (Matsumoto, 2019).

We should set a plan for the future of our generations. They will be our future engineers, doctors, builders etc.... Their careers are molded by the educators of today. Together, the education system will eventually reform itself to better serve humanity. With the right values we teach our students and with empowering educators who have the knowledge and the know-how, we can set the pace for the reform of education, as UAE envisioned it.

"Anyone who stops learning is old, whether at twenty or eighty. Anyone who keeps learning stays young. The greatest thing in life is to keep your mind young."
– Henry Ford Quotes

Set a Plan for Future and Career

Why should we set plans? The whole procedure is intended to move you forward in life, building yourself a superior future. However, how do you start planning such a feat? There are many books that emphasizing for individual to set a plan for their future. However, it not necessary to do what precisely the book says. When book direct the reader that they have to write goals in a piece of paper, put it order from highest priority to the lowest, then set a target and a deadline to make it more realistic. Simply, it is smart to do like the book describe but you can only take a few minutes to think about it.

    A great advice is after you have thought of your goal, it is ideal to put it on a piece of paper therefore it is obvious for you. Also, what I do for example is that if I have a goal like opening a business or studying for an important exam, I will write the target (I want to get X profit in the first year, I want X mark in the exam) on a sticky note and hang it on the wall, mirror, or a pinboard. Anywhere you know it can be seen every day therefore it reminds and stimulate the subconscious mind part of your brain to reach your target. In your mind, it is trustworthy to set a deadline and put a realistic timeline as some goals take longer than you expect, which is typical.

According to Dr. Gabriele Oettingen, "If the future is indeed perceived as bright as these findings suggest, then thinking about the future should encourage a positive, optimistic outlook and an eagerness to pursue rewards despite the risks." Furthermore, it's clever when you set your goals you put for yourself other options next to your main goal. Therefore, that will reduce stress while you're trying to reach the first option. Also, it will ease the as you have other options on side.

Planning for your future and for your career is vital if you want to advance. That could clear your way and you vision. Also, it accelerates and save time as you have it clear in front. Using SMART approach which refer to (S – Specific, M – Measurable, A – Attainable, R – Relevant and T – Timely). A created plan can be Specific and include a timeline – making it informal to measure your accomplishment. You will be able to rapidly see if your plan is achievable given the approach and timeline you are giving yourself and the consequence of each step will become clear. Using this strategy for study and other goals could support achieving your target.

As mentioned earlier in regards of setting your goals, it's smart to plan the negatives as well. A written plan will force you to concenter on your complete goals and not just your instant plans. You will have the time and time frame you want to be in at each stage of your career. However, you will need to build well as a 'what if' factor – not every phase along the way will be full of roses and rainbows. It's difficult and very challenging, but forecasts and plans can also be made for them; the below-suggested plan you could use that list all possible obstacles, concerns, or challenges you face in accomplishing your career plan:

- List all things that can go wrong with the plan.
- Create a positive response to each of these negatives that you have recognized.
- Conserve your reactions, information, thoughts, and resources so that if these negative aspects exist, you are ready for unexpected events.

Being organized and preparing for the negatives will turn them into possible to reach the goal. Learning experiences that are just setbacks along the way. Can slow you down a bit, but you never lose the plan and save time.

Picturing your goals, writing it down, and planning for any challenge in your way could double increase the chance of reaching the targets faster and peaceful. That will keep you focused, motivated, and mindfulness as the steps planned and cleared.

H.H. Sheikh Mohammed bin Rashid Al Maktoum in his twitter account said about planning for future, "The future belongs to those who can imagine it, design it, and execute it. It isn't something you await, but rather create."

" صناعة المستقبــــل لا تبنى على الاحتمالات والأرقام بقـــــدر التخطيط والتنفيذ "

Generating an alternative plan that has been prepared might save time and the most popular methods for emerging alternatives through brainstorming. An individual or team works organized to develop ideas and alternative solutions to a better outcome.

Therefore, **this advice for my beloved nieces, nephews, and everyone reading my book,** I believe that you have something different, talent, and individuality that's only meant for you; search for it deep inside, and you will find it. Be proud of whatever you are and what you have, and make sure to do something unique that makes you happiest person in the world and your beloved one.

By Dr. Areej ElSayary

Why we should set a plan for future and career?

Due to the lockdown caused by the COVID-19, millions of workers have experienced changes that transformed their lives, well-being, and productivity that impacted economies and labor markets. Many questions were raised about individuals' future and career, the use of technology needed, modern communication, and online learning. Will we have the same jobs after ten or twenty years? What competencies are needed for the demands of the new jobs that do not yet exist? What will learning look like after COVID-19? How can students' cognitive, social, and emotional skills be developed? How can students' engagement in online learning be enhanced? How can teaching and learning presence be promoted in online learning?

Developing and enhancing learners' knowledge and skills are key drivers to produce quality, skillful workers with adequate employability skills. The global shift to a future of work is defined by an ever-expanding cohort of new technologies that are more interconnected where information and knowledge are widely spread. Applied technology is considered an effective tool to facilitate the teaching and learning process to create an active learning environment in an era of online and blended learning. This includes the elements of organizing an active learning environment using applied technology: learning sciences and teamwork, communication and creation, personalization of learning, critical thinking, and real-world engagement. Accordingly, it will lead to the development of learners' digital competencies that prepare skilled workers for the new market needs.

In response to the COVID-19 pandemic, schools and universities in UAE had to shift to emergence remote teaching. Accordingly, many gaps occurred concerning online engagement and students' learning environments. Efforts were made to restructure the instructional design of the courses to be suitable for online learning. Schools and universities across UAE adopted different communication platforms such as Zoom, Adobe Connect, Microsoft Teams, etc. As a result of the lockdown, the learning plans in schools and universities were changed to fit the remote learning. There is currently no literature about the learning and working after COVID-19. Many questions were raised in different webinars about online/hybrid learning, future jobs needed, competencies, and students' wellbeing.

Students usually develop their understanding of the world when a potential change to their perspectives and frames of reference occurred. It has been stated that students can transform their learning when they are placed in an uncomfortable situation (Strange and Gibson, 2017). The lockdown of the COVID-19 that happened in March 2020 is considered an uncomfortable situation for instructors and preservice teachers. Transformative learning is based on Dewey's (1933) pragmatic aesthetics and application of learning to learners' everyday life and experience where students should be involved in real-life tasks that require integrated disciplines and critical reflection (Singelton, 2015). Orr (1992) claims that transformative learning requires integrated disciplines and the intellect, emotion, and body, focusing on the cognitive, affective, and psychomotor domains. The Head, Heart, and Hand model represented by Orr (1992) sets out an effective pedagogy that brings real life to the curriculum and learning environment, which requires students to be engaged in critical thinking, rational discourse, and transform their perspectives to solve ill-structured problems (Singelton, 2015).

This model implies considering three important learning domains (cognitive, affective, and psychomotor) in creating the instructional activities that enhance students' engagements. It will focus on a strong pedagogy that develops students' critical thinking, self-direction, communication, collaboration, creativity and innovation, and problem-solving skills. Borup *et al.,* (2020) emphasized the importance of considering the three factors of students' engagements (cognitive, affective, and behavior) in the instructional design of the online courses. Furthermore, feedback is an essential factor that fosters students' engagement in online learning through a culminating instructional design framework (Czerkawski and Lyman, 2016).

"The function of education is to teach one to think intensively and to think critically. Intelligence plus character – that is the goal of true education."

– Martin Luther King, Jr.

Time Management

In the section, we'll discuss time management definition and will look at a small study done by the author. The keywords always come with time management are planning, prioritization, procrastination, production, deadline, and timetable. Time management is a skill and progression of developing and directing the time consumed on specific activities, particularly to expansion effectiveness, efficiency, and productivity of the day or a task. It is about meeting various demands of an individual regarding the job, study, community, household, interests, individual interests, and obligations with the boundedness of time. Roda Ayane mentioned in an article, "Time management is a priority-based structuring of time allocation and distribution among competing demands since time cannot be stored, and its availability can neither be increased beyond nor decrease from the 24 hours." Ayane continued it's crucial as being and material resource in any association for the researcher, academic performance, and work performance.

On 19 August 2021, a small study conducted by Alriyami; Hajer included only one question sent to 150 participants through social media in UAE. She collected 102 responses. The target of this small study is workers and (student and worker) therefore will look at people who are studying and engaged with work and family. To look at it from their perspective and how they manage their time. Below we'll look at the question and at time management from two angles: students and (students and workers) with facts.

1) Are you? (Worker), (Student and Worker)

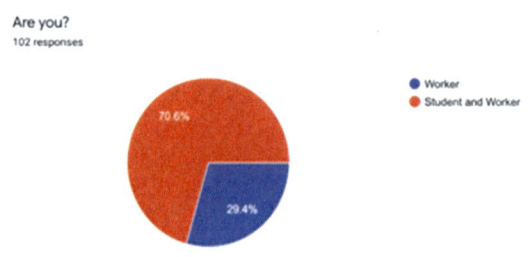

Figure 1. shows 29% of the participant's workers and 70% (Student and Worker).

2) Marital Status: (Single), (Married)

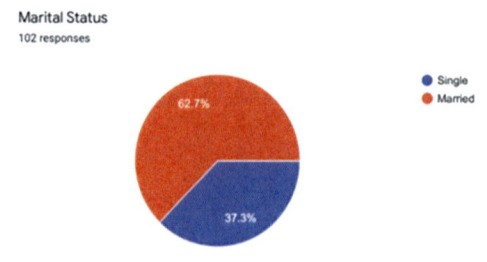

Figure 2. shows 37% of the participants are single and 62% married.

3) Do you think you have enough time daily to complete your tasks?

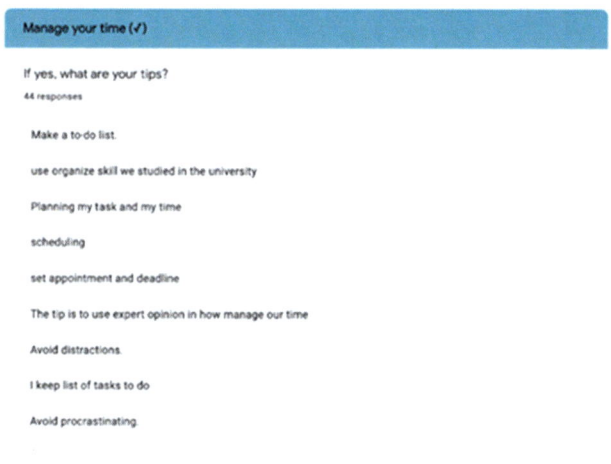

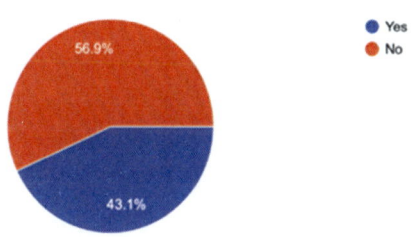

Figure 3. shows that 43% of the participants answered yes, and 56% answered, no.

If yes, what are your tips?

Manage your time (✘)

If no, why, and what is your strategy to manage your time?
58 responses

setup another appointment in the calendar

less working hours

professional training

I try to use weekly planner

don't take another task till you finish the one you have

start with important staff

You probably are overloading yourself with too many tasks in one session. You can take one experience at a task and adjust for future tasks. For example, you spent about 1 hour on this one task today despite planning it for 30 minutes.

Finish the more important things first then less important

Figure 4 shows 44 of the participants answered yes, about half of them married, and the other half are single. Correspondingly, the fascinating, amazing fact is more the majorly 30 out of 44 are student and worker plus 20 out of 44 are married though they were able to manage their time. They believe it is to keep a list of tasks to do and it could support managing the time effectively. Also, they recommended to set goal, scheduling and planning to follow, always prioritize everting, divide the tasks, assess the value of your tasks, calculate the time spent on each of your tasks, give each tasks a time to work on, use weekly planner and project tool, exercises, use google or apple calendar, teamwork if needed with your coworker, set appointment and deadline, record everything down in order, avoid distractions and procrastinating, be flexible adaptable to know when to cut, and use expert opinion in how manage our time. Participants' tips support my advice in the book, particularly the last tip.

If no, why, and what is your strategy to manage your time?

Figure 5 shows 58 of the participants answered no, 44 out of 58 majority are married, and only 14 out of 58 are single. Correspondingly, 41 out 58 are student and worker and 17 out 58 workers. It reasonable that they couldn't manage their time as they are working, studying, and parenting simultaneously. The participant's strategy or suggestion to maximize productivity is as follow. They suggested decreasing working hours to have more time for other tasks and home. They also suggested to set time and deadline, use checklist to organize task, reschedule, don't take another task till you finish the one you have, explain to others why you can't take more tasks by showing your timetable project, underestimating how much time you need and maybe not being fully focused on the tasks do a weekly planner, focus on my current responsibilities and make sure my to-do list is my main priority, tasks are not clear therefore approach line manager or colleagues for more exaptation. Moreover, some of responds show that participants don't have clear vision or strategy to complete their task.

I found two interesting responds to the above question. First, the participant suggested to learn to say a 'no' to people many times it gets stimulating for people to say a 'no' to events which unexpectedly come their way, which disturbs their agenda. Do not take distractions your way. Focus on one activity at a time instead of doing parallel multi-tasking.

Indeed, as it mentioned above show other that are not able to handle more project as you have schedule and deadline to meet. In this way, others will respect and understand your position.

Another participant suggested professional training to organize time well. Taking training from an expert could support managing your task and boost your performance at your firm. In another word, time management training is an ability that can develop numerous qualities of your work life. It supports to be more efficient and effective by allowing you to complete more tasks in less time a day. Other benefits of learning this skill and incorporating time management into your life or work involve:

- Extend free time
- Advance productivity and less stress
- Enhance decision-making ability
- Enhance professional standing
- Enhance ability to focus longer on professionals' matter
- Enhance parallel of self-discipline
- Increase professional growth and progress and its opportunities.

Summary of the modest study: People are becoming more aware of their needs and researching the goal from different angles before joining the program, such as family, financial matter, time matter (classes schedule), Covid-19 matter (study abroad). However, I also notice that there are a good number of people who don't measure everything; for example, in the middle of the program, they are in a financial crisis where they should be stable and aware of the cost. Moreover, sometimes students enter with the condition, and they know that they will be held for a document at any time. Example of missing document are degree, certificate attestation, ID, or required test. They leave it until the end, and they don't follow with the enrollment office, which leaves them stressed and unmotivated to study with energy.

Therefore, my advice is don't put yourself in this position and wait for it till the last minutes crucial decision. As I mentioned, measure everything and all steps, even if that will take from you more time to be able to study with stress-free, energy, and complete focus only in the program. This is what I did to feel comfortable during the study, and I tried to make sure nothing would stop me from completing my courses. What do you think; is it worth it to lose time for a better study environment?

"An investment in knowledge pays the best interest."
— Benjamin Franklin

Health and Education

Here I would like to highlight the point about the link between our health condition (sickness, chronic disease, learning disability cases, etc.) with completing education and does it impact on one's education, life, and career. Also, will share people thoughts who have the knowledge in this area such us Dr. Efthymia. I believe that there is positive relation between our health condition and completing education. In fact, your educational journey depends on whom you are studying with and who are your colleagues. Also, depending on the people if they highly take in consideration that others were born special and need help in some areas. The awareness of understanding that they need to be treated depending on their case whether it was for their physical need, emotional need, or both. The idea of integrating these cases with students make them feel not different is an amazing idea not only for special cases but also for the students to learn to accept everyone as they are.

From my humble experience dealing with cases, I noticed that although students suffered and had to face these critical problems and study in a bad environment, they are the ones most caring; they respond quickly and are willing to do the impossible to complete their educational journey. Therefore, those blessed with a better environment, knowledge, skill, and time and who have full support, why not use these privileges to enjoy the journey or complete our journey?

A great example to add in this section would be Chaica Al Qassimi. She was born with Down syndrome, and she only came to know about her condition when she turned 21. She represents UAE Inclusion Ambassador and Youth Leader and worked in nine jobs. She proved that there is no barrier when it comes to disability. She shows how strong and determined people have to overcome their difficulties and, as she said, get included and united with others in her interview with Anas Bukhas. Al Qassimi: "People with disabilities are amazing, and I want them to not be alone in the world," says the award-winning athlete. Besides Al Qassimi, there are millions of notable honored examples whose stories and accomplishments won't fit my book.

By Dr. Efthymia Efthymiou

Abstract

For centuries, society tended to see disability as a deity cut off from other social issues. Stigma and prejudice against people with disabilities were the strongest barriers to integration, equal opportunities, and equal access to education, employment, health, and leisure. Special education programs and legislation for people with disabilities, ensure their autonomy, professional integration, and participation in the social, economic, and political life of the country. Following the international trends, the UAE promotes equal access for people of determination in all areas of social life. Although the elimination of marginalization and exclusion is a key human rights issue, the declarations are not enough. The main reason for the social exclusion of people with disabilities is the existence of stereotypes and negative prejudices of the social environment, which come from lack of awareness about disability issues.

Introduction

The term disability refers to limitations of speech, actions, or direct perceptions due to physical or mental injury of a person (Patel and Brown, 2017). Disability is one of the most widely discussed issues in society. Its conceptual definition differs across countries. The international literature mentions many different definitions, which have been given by sociologists, psychologists, doctors, biologists, educators, etc. Most definitions are medically oriented which emphasize the deviation of the person from 'normal,' while they fail to underline the social factors that define disability. According to the definition of the UN Social and Economic Council, 'a disabled person is any person who cannot meet all or part of the needs of a normal individual or social life due to congenital or acquired physical or intellectual disability' (Schur, Kruse, and Blanck, 2013).

Social exclusion encompasses concepts of inequality, poverty, and segregation (Bernt and Colini, 2013). Large sections of the population, including the disabled, are excluded from their participation in economic, social, political, and cultural life and tend to be marginalized in society. Disability is a social construct that changes over time and with it, the way people with disabilities are treated by their environment. In modern times, the exclusion and 'special' treatment experienced by people with disabilities are serious social issues. The existence of social exclusion violates the human rights of people with disabilities and deprives their right to actively participate in community and society.

Discrimination has been described by European law as injustice, and scientific community is investigating the matter to eliminate stigma and prejudice (Corrigan and Shapiro, 2010). Although many steps forward have been made in recent decades, with the recognition of the disability movement, the institutionalization of their rights and the implementation of programs, the social inclusion of people with disabilities has not progressed satisfactorily. To drastically change the current situation on how people with disabilities are treated and the perceptions around them to achieve effective integration and reintegration of people with disabilities, it is necessary to follow an active policy tool for the full implementation of the United Nations Convention on the Rights of Persons with Disabilities.

A Social View of Disability

The theoretical starting point of the social model of disability is found in Britain by activists and students in the 1970s, in the formation of the Union of Physically Impaired Against Segregation, questioning the medical model of disability and its definitions of disability (Crow, 2010). The distinction between impairment and disability is a central point of the social model. The concept of impairment refers to impaired use of limbs, impaired mental and intellectual abilities of the person, including dysfunctions of the internal organs of the body. On the other hand, disability, refers to the limitations encountered by a person with disability, caused by society when does not provide the necessary support to become functional.

The social model answers the question 'what causes disability?' emphasizing not the medical factors, but considering the environmental, psychological, cultural, and social factors. It does not deny the problem of disability but, contrary to the medical model, it ceases to incriminate the individual and responsibility is sought in society (Oliver, 2018). It places disability not in an incapacitated or dysfunctional body, but in a prohibitive and oppressive social environment, and argues that many of the limitations imposed on people with disabilities are not a normal or inevitable consequence of their disability, but a product of social environment. The social model explains the difficulties experienced by people with disabilities based on the ways society is structured and disability is constructed. It is not the individual constraints that cause the problem but the failure of society to provide the appropriate services to people with disabilities.

Disability is not a characteristic of the individual but a complex set of conditions. Society renders people disabled by excluding them from the right to full participation in social life and places them in a marginal position of dependence, poverty, unemployment, and the denial of equal rights to which they are entitled as citizens. The model views disability through the barriers that a person needs to overcome to participate equally in society. They are all those things that impose restrictions on people with disabilities, taking as a point of reference the model of a 'normal person' and continuing with individual prejudices, negative behaviors, stigmatization, and discrimination. The various obstacles, economic, political, and social, place people with disabilities at the top of the problem, in a way that isolates them and excludes them from full participation in society.

The social model of disability focuses on the changes that are needed in society, such as having a more positive attitude toward people with disabilities, eliminating underestimation, fear, and negativism (Nario-Redmond, 2019). Shifting the center of gravity from the individual to the social level had multiple implications. In contrast to the medical model, which encourages prejudices, stigma, and exclusion of people with disabilities, the social model has a positive approach and places particular emphasis on the terms, appropriate, reasonable, integrated, and accepted. It stresses that disability does not imply the loss of potential, productivity, ability to contribute to society, and that disability is part of human life. Its purpose is to eliminate the stigma and alienation, which are often experienced by a person with disability.

The implementation of this model implies significant benefits for society, with the active participation of people with disabilities in social life, mainly through education and through the open labor market. A precondition for achieving this is for society to learn to value difference and to embrace that all differences have a role to play in the social system.

Disabled people are not a single, cohesive social group with common interests and visions; nor do they share a common fate, that of apostasy and deprivation, but they experience similar situations that contribute to their exclusion, e.g., social, educational, etc. People with disabilities are exposed to negative social behaviors that have serious consequences both physically and psychologically. This significantly reduces the opportunities to be productive members of society and increases the risk of being trapped in poverty (Devandas Aguilar, 2017). This degrading psychological process is the beginning of a vicious cycle of discrimination. Stereotypes, prejudices, social constructions about the characteristics of an individual or a group do not allow individuals to maintain their place in collective life, resulting in psychological consequences, which create anxiety and fear.

Disability and Education

Education is an important factor where it leads to marginalization and social exclusion. Their relationship is endless. They were linked by the Council of Europe when addressing the issue of social exclusion based on five areas of social life: education, housing, social protection, employment, and health (Allen, Cars, and Madanipour, 2012). Infrastructure shortages in the current education system perpetuate educational inequalities and cause a kind of educational exclusion that reproduces situations of social exclusion especially for those whose access to higher education is restricted. It is known that the school frees the child from principles and prejudices. The education system, while by its very nature contributes to social inclusion, but for some sections of the population functions as a mechanism of social exclusion. Children from socially excluded groups are at a greater risk of experiencing social exclusion from education. In fact, most young people who drop out of school come from families with a low socio-economic and educational level (Tranter, 2012).

Starting from the democratic principle 'everyone has the right to be different from others,' the school considers individual differences, without dividing children into categories, but in carefully identifying individual abilities (Jonassen and Grabowski, 2012). Democratic philosophy implies the concept that all children should be given the opportunity to learn, whether they are children without educational or social problems, or highly gifted, mentally retarded, blind, deaf, emotionally disturbed, children with multiple disabilities. The right to education is a central point in the exercise of social rights because its deprivation is an essential obstacle to their exercise. From 1959 until today, there have been several declarations and conventions on the rights of persons with disabilities in education (Munyi, 2012). The way people with disabilities are treated is an example of a country's culture. And it should all start at school. These are all subjects of education. The school should inspire respect for people with disabilities. Unfortunately, however, the education system is so constructed that it does not offer substantial education and training to its future citizens, to accept the disabled, as their equal fellow citizens.

To promote equality in education, it is crucial to be aware of the importance of ensuring access to education (Pazey and Cole, 2013). It is now accepted that to promote equality in education, it is not enough just to ensure access to and participation in the education system, but also to have the necessary conditions for a substantial degree of success for all those involved in the education system. These two views are an expression of different perceptions of the causes of inequality, which affect society's responsibility to promote equality in education.

Staying Positive Despite Disability

People with disabilities internationally, especially in Western culture, are provided with support through state care, to get educated and becoming autonomous for integrating into society smoothly. People with disabilities may have one or more difficulties or deficiencies, but in most cases, according to international research, they will excel and have a more developed characteristic or ability (Whyte and Ingstad, 2020). There are examples of individuals, who at times were characterized as special, excelled, or emerged because of a particular characteristic or ability. Typical examples are Newton and Einstein, who were found to have Asperger's Syndrome, an Autism syndrome in which people have autistic features but are highly functional and highly intelligent. Nevertheless, these two people excelled in the Positive Sciences, to the extent of influencing humanity, indefinitely. Other examples include Beethoven, the deaf musician who excelled in his compositions; Frida Kahlo, a woman who created unique paintings; Ellen Keller, the blind and deaf author, with 12 books to her credit; and Marla Ranian, the athlete, who won four medals at the Paralympic Games.

The examples are endless, especially nowadays, where the support received by many people with disabilities helps them to develop their positive abilities and characteristics. Moreover, in some areas they show developed skills. For example, people with autism usually have a developed interest and ability to use new technology media, such as computers and any media with images (Mintz, and Aagaard, 2012). This means that these people with the right support and training can become creative and useful to society, filling in positions and providing services that require technological knowledge (World Health Organization, 2019). This example shows that people with disabilities can no longer be considered 'special.' If the positive abilities that these individuals have are highlighted, they can become autonomous, useful, and productive members of society. Education and support for these individuals should start early in their lives bearing in mind that some other ability or characteristic will develop. It is this finding that will lead not only to the improvement of the quality of life of these individuals, but also to their acceptance by the general society.

People of determination are vivid examples of willingness to remain active citizens with courage and patience in the face of their challenges. They do not want comfort, nor do they need pity. They need, like everyone else, sincere love and selfless interest. It is no coincidence that in the most modern definitions and categorizations of people with disabilities, gifted people with high intelligence and functionality are included, as they also need special support and training, to maintain and further develop their high functionality (Subotnik, Olszewski-Kubilius, and Worrell, 2011). People with disabilities are 'people first' (Halmari, 2011). Society's behaviors should offer them equal and full participation in family and social life and the possibility of co-decision, in issues that affect their life and future. Attitudes that inspire respect and trust, embrace diversity.

"Don't stop when you're tired, stop when you're don't."
– Wesley Snipes

Why I Need a Higher Qualification?

This topic has always been an arguable subject when the conversation as follows. First person: I'm going to complete my master's program. Second person: oh, good to hear. In what? First person: not sure. I will meet the adviser to discuss that. Second person: though it won't benefit you here, they don't support the promoting system. Now I can leave you to continue the conversation and reply to the second person. My reply to the second person will be, don't limit yourself with the company you're working in and move out of your zone and search for a career opportunity outside your company if yours doesn't support promoting system. The most important thing is don't move before you secure yourself even if it took a long period of time.

I always believe that the master's program is ideal for everyone to set in long-term goals, though many people disagree. I think it could be an opportunity you could find one day that needs this qualification. Chances don't appear every day, and it will not wait for you to complete the requirement of fitting the position. Now that I graduated with a master's degree, it opened the door to understand many concepts that it was unidentified. It also gives me the confidence to complete my doctoral program.

This approves that everyone needs to work in both qualifications and experience as extremely important for applying for any position. What I'm trying to point out that be better than the second person with unconvincing excuses like promoting system, lack of time, or any other endless reasons. I'm hoping for you when you read this section that you're convinced enough to complete your higher education. I believe that every excuse has a solution, and you can work it out one by one. You're the one who can decide whether this excuse could stay as a barrier from enhancing and develop yourself, or you're the one who can break it like I did. As I mentioned earlier, let me summarize why we need higher qualification for the following reasons.

1. To enlarge the number of chances to experience another career opportunity.
2. Expand of knowledge and idea for the study.
3. Better communication with others because of the variety of ideas and knowledge.
4. To increase the individual income.
5. Better security as what in your hand may not take to a higher level (professionally).
6. A role module of encouragement for younger people your (sister, brother, daughter, son, cousin, or a friend).
7. Self-development and enhance skills like critical thinking, problem solving, management, and leading.

Another debatable subject about qualifications is (what is more critical qualifications or experience). Andrew Main is Vice Dean of Bournemouth University. He believes that qualifications speak more about people than their academic ability. First and foremost, he would want to emphasize that a degree is not solely for the purpose of obtaining employment or a career. Intellectual, social, athletic, personal, artistic, ethical, and many other aspects of life are all affected by benefits. Recruiters frequently state in job postings that a degree is required, so the market establishes and evaluates the degree.

In addition, he mentioned, "Today. So I have more work than I did 50 years ago; I have to work with my brain and minor job with manual skills." After all, a degree is the start of a professional career, followed by its credibility. Giving a decent place will create more and more options for a person's future development. He compared equivalent information and give an example, a 21-year-old graduate compared with a 21-year-old with industry experience. Both experienced 21-year-old graduates have equal intelligence. Let me respect that experience: it does not erase the intelligence (like some scholars, they assume the opposite). But education changes you.

Furthermore, given that the same time has passed, education will bring a more profound understanding than the experience can provide. Therefore, from experience, you may discover that this does not work, but education provides you with theoretical knowledge and analytical abilities, as well as an explanation for why it does not. Furthermore, education improves your learning speed as well as your ability to study thoroughly. As a result, seasoned professionals will pick up new ideas for procedures and technologies.

From my perspective, I think both are equally important for self-development. Earning a degree means moving to a high position. This position required advanced skills such as analyzing data, critical thinking, reflecting, negotiation, etc. These skills need someone with higher qualifications and broader knowledge to drive the company toward better performance.

Final Thoughts

It is coming to the end of section one that highlighted the essentials of education in many aspects and different approaches. Final thoughts I would encourage everyone to complete high education when they see that you have time, knowledge (skills), and ability use this chance that might come once in your life. The best feeling when you have something valuable in your hand that makes you proud. **Beyond doubt, highly confined that at the moment you already have existed valued thing in your hand, and you are looking to shine more and more.** The following section of the book might change your mind, and I hope it encourages you to complete your higher education.

Express your thoughts them with me by the end of the book.

_____
_____
_____
_____
_____
_____
_____
_____

Section Two
My Educational Journey

Let me start by defining it, as an educational journey, not only experience you have from preschool to the present (the last program you are enrolled in). However, it also involves the steps you took from registration to apply for graduation, the friendship you make with everyone in the institution, and the different emotions you get during your journey. Indeed, one thing to remember is despite the qualification we have, learning should be a non-stop journey and it must be available for everyone.

This section I will talk about my educational journey, experience, and sharing stories that happened in school and mostly in university. Also, in this section, I will provide some recommendations for people who are thinking of pursuing higher education that could support them and made their journey flatter. That was the purpose of this section as I always feel that it's challenging for students to find someone, not necessarily a professional but someone like a joiner who is willing to talk and share the best advice for them to choose to form their options or a solution.

My journey from what I remember were primarily positive. It had vacillation like anyone's journey and isn't significant like Oprah Winfrey or other celebrities; however, I decided to put it in one place for you and hoping you will enjoy it.

"Education is the ability to listen to almost anything without losing your temper or your self-confidence."
— Robert Frost

Before Joining the School

At this stage, age 4-6 years, what I will share is from my blurry memory and what my parents told me. I was diagnosed with Turner Syndrome around 1997 and mine was very light appeared only two symptoms as it was tough to notice it, and there was a rare case in the UAE, and I was the second case by that time. From Healthline newspaper, medically reviewed by Dr. Alana Biggers, she graduated from the University of Illinois at Chicago, specializes in internal medicine. In addition, an interview was conducted via phone with Dr. Mohamed Wasfi El Abiary specializes consultant pediatric endocrinologist. Turner syndrome is a genetic condition caused by an abnormality on one of your sex chromosomes; only the female sex develops this condition. It's also called monosomy X, gonadal dysgenesis, and Bonnevie-Ullrich syndrome. Turner syndrome occurs when part or all of one of your X chromosomes is missing. This condition affects approximately one in 2,000 females. People with Turner syndrome can lead healthy lives. However, they typically require some consistent, ongoing medical supervision to detect and treat complications.

Before I was diagnosed in 1994, Dr. Abduallah Azam, a pediatrician his colleague, noticed and informed Dr. Azam about me, that we were visiting him only for a regular checkup. Dr. Azam remarked that I have (TS) is impossible as he couldn't see any sign, and I was highly typical like other children in my age except that I was marginally shorter. Pediatricians know that (TS) has many symptoms and causes congenital malformation such as in the heart, neck, hands, etc. However, in my case, only 1-2 of the signs were shown, and it was unnoticeable.

My doctor took a blood sample and sent it outside to London for the test as in past they didn't have this kind of test here, and no availability of the medicine as there were only one case by that time. After days and weeks of waiting, the results come back positive from London. The doctor called my father and have to deliver the sad news. At the same time, he has to send a memo to order treatment called growth hormone. My father was shocked by the news to him practicality after six healthy kids with rare case asking three doctors besides Dr. Azam to confirm the diagnosis and treatment.

Despite the fact that my father's job was important as a police officer, he requested to travel to the United States (Cleveland Hospital) seeking better treatment for his daughter, which was in 1998. I was fortunate that my mum went to medical school; though they did not teach her how to inject needles because she didn't complete her study; she has a background. I had to take this treatment every day, and I remember I was eager to learn how to inject a needle that one day I observed my mother. The needles weren't the type of pen developed like nowadays; I was frightened to try but curious. The next day, I took the needle, cleaned the area, and I injected myself, and I walked away like nothing happened.

Not certain that day if my mother injected me again and I took overdoses.

"The more that you read, the more things you will know, the more that you learn, the more places you'll go."

– Dr. Seuss

Primary School

After all that, my parents had to register me for school after a long trip. It was challenging for them because the school read my file and decided to put me in the 'special class' with other kids who were special cases. In fact, it wasn't a usual case to my parents, like a fever or inflammation. However, they rejected the school's decision and tried to persuade them to try first year (1st grade) in normal class. The school agreed and accepted my parents' decision not to put me in the 'special class.' I faced troubles as I was a hyperactive kid and my mum had to stay in the class to observe me from a distance. Everything went well in the first year, and I learned what I needed to move to 2nd grade. Surely, my parents were happy that their daughter was finally stable and on the track. I have been told I did great till the 3rd grade. Suddenly, I refused to join my class, and whenever my mum put me in the class, I cried as something scary happened hysterically in the class and every time, I ran to the administration building. That continued for weeks and weeks. Imagine that the school is far from home. This led to my father's late arrival to work because they called my parents and informed them that your daughter is sitting in the administration office refusing to join the class, then he has to drop Mother at the school. Can you guess what happened since till the moment, no one knows what happened in the classroom.

I can't put words together what my parents had to go through to support me throughout my educational journey. I can't imagine how they have the power how to manage six kids with adding a sick daughter and the things they went through till today. I would say that my parents had invested in my siblings and me well. **This message is for all parents;** thank you for being a great mother, and father keeps trying to provide the best for your children as one day you will see it reflecting on them.

"Educating the mind without educating the heart is no education at all."

– Aristotle

What Happened Next?

Every day, the hospital's tests and results improved with the treatment for the next six years. The teacher in the school was happy with my performance and grade. I finally got to live normally like other kids, and my hospital appointments became less and less. Also, the reduction of calls to my parent from the school. That put them in a break from missive trips between the hospital, school, and back to home in the afternoon till what happened next. In September 2005, I started to get weaker; I lost appetite to eat that counted for approximately one month until my father decided before visiting the park pass by the clinic to run some test. The result comes back. On 5 December 2005, I was diagnosed with diabetes type 1. Now I must visit the hospital more frequently because the rustles average for the past three months was terrifically high 16, and the target should be 4-6.

In the beginning, I was hospitalized a lot, and every time I learned how to control my blood sugar levels. I remember one of the times I was tremendously sick that I couldn't walk, and I was bothered and weeping from the hospital wires all around my arm and chest to monitor my heart condition as it wasn't stable. I'm glad that my condition wasn't worse than I thought that wouldn't stop me from finishing school or miss classes at the university.

The message here for people with a case similar to mine and people with any sickness or chronic disease is, believe me, that you have double the power of others who are healthy. Also, the advice is to start with your capacity or standard and then slightly raise it. For instance, if your capacity is to run three km daily, train yourself marginally to reach your target.

"Education is what remains after one has forgotten what one has learned in school."

– Albert Einstein

Where the Challenges Started

I spent the first year of university fine and learning the new system. Moving from school life to university where things were forbidden and not allowed, like using the phone in the classroom and permission to leave the classroom. I had a great true friend that our friendship didn't end until today, almost nine years.

To where the challenges start, I graduated with a double major business and IT diploma. The graduation required a test to earn the degree. I passed the test on the third attempt. I thought the summer would be a relaxing time and have some quality time with the family.

However, summer 2012 was full of tests such as math and English test to enter the bachelor program. The website and library are full of resources for the test; however, I didn't know why I made such a mistake in the practices as I need help from the expert. Finally, after four attempts that took approximately three to four months, I got the required score. The registration closed, and I couldn't join the university in the first semester for the bachelor program because I took the test in October. I had to wait until mid-November; therefore, I enrolled in the second half of the academic year, February 2013.

The message here for everyone fighting their dream. Keep trying different strategies till you find the way that works for you. This is what I did, and this is my advice to you. Think out of the box, try to take one step out of your comfort zone, and try something different. No matter how long your dreams take, days, months, years keep fighting back; you will see it one day. It took me one year and a half to achieve my dream, others less, or maybe more; the point is to keep fighting.

"Intellectual growth should commence at birth and cease only at death."

– Albert Einstein

The Most Frightening Experience Happened in My Life

Finally, I have five months to rest before the semester start, and I decided to use this time to focuses on my health. Exercises and sport are one thing to do for my health at home or going to the gym. Another thing is to force me to drink more water to hydrate my body. I tried to socialize more with my family because the summer took me away from them. Now that I have time, I decided to get a driving license.

On 22 October 2012, I went to Saudi Arabia to perform 'Hajj.' I traveled with my father, cousin, and uncle. I thought it would be crowded with people like what I have seen in media and TV, but it was organized, and everything went smoothly. We spent eight days performing 'Hajj' on the last day when the most frightening thing happened.

On our way by bus from Makkah to Jeddah, I was tired, and had a snack. I injected myself with insulin, though I shouldn't because my blood sugar levels were almost low. We arrived at Jeddah 7:00 am in the early morning and our flight was at 7:00 pm in the evening. I saw the bag full of food and snacks on my way into the bedroom, and I said, "I have plenty of time; let me first sleep." This was the last thing I said before I went into a diabetes coma for around 10 to 12 hours.

I was sleeping, and my cousin did not know that my sugar is going down. She woke me up several times, and I was barely moving until she has no response. She called my father and told him that I wasn't moving or responding to her call. I was a body without a soul, my father tapped my shoulder and my hand fell. Everyone was scared thinking I was dead. My father carried me to the lobby asking for the nearest emergency room. The receptionist provided a wheelchair and pointed it out to him, saying, "Uncle, here the next building you can find the hospital." I was fortunate that our hotel was right next to the hospital, minutes of walking. My uncle checked my sugar; it was 50 mg/dl before my father took me to the hospital. ER nurses were shocked when they saw my father. My father went to the reception desk asked for registration. The doctor shouted, "Later," asking, "what she has and how this happened." The only thing my father could think of at that moment was 'she has diabetic.'

A smart decision from the doctor gave me glucose Intravenous through the IV line till the blood test come from the lab. When I entered the hospital, my sugar was 25 mg/dl, and the doctor said that I'm a second away from a brain stroke or bleeding. I woke up approximately 25 minutes after medicine worked. I felt my father's hand massaging my hand. That made a confusion that I felt between dream and real I kept asking him, "Dad, am I dreaming? Where are we?"

After I woke up, the doctor asked me couple of questions and my blood sugar levels went normal. My father asked, "Now three hours to our flight. Are you fine? Would you be able to travel?"

I saw the concern on his face. I answered immediately, "Yes, yes, we can." I stood up from the bed. I wanted to show him that I'm fine. Each one of these sicknesses and challenges has made me stronger and ready to fight more enormous.

"To teach is to learn twice."
— Joseph Joubert

To the Last Step Before My Next Journey

I thought of completing my master's degree in the same area (business). After graduation, I spent one-year resting, reading books, and socializing with my family. In January 2018, I got hired for my first career in my life as an administrative. I enjoyed and still enjoying my job supporting my colleagues. In year 2019 during summer, I thought of joining the university to complete my master's degree. Some requirements stopped me; however, I kept trying until I passed the test after eight attempts. I tried online resources, book guidance, face-to-face class, all options. I'm glad at the end I met Ms. Cathy. She was friendly, willing to teach from scratch, and highly patient with me.

    These required tests made me avoid reading as I tried to focus and practice for the test. That might be why I feel unpleasant when reading the book and prevent me from enhancing my reading skill. The issue I'm trying to point out is a struggle with reading or finding an interesting subject. Recently, I have been trying to look for similar books that I read, and I like them to educate and improve my reading skill. Dear reader, if you face this kind of issue, try till you find yourself like reading one day. Then, allocate time for reading that could help, for example, before bedtime or after breakfast with a cup of coffee.

For both bachelor and the master's degree, I felt I fought and broke the strongest wall I would ever face in my life. In the end, the best thing is the taste of success after experiencing failure. Keep in mind, without challenges, we won't feel the taste of success and happiness. After one year and a half, I finally enrolled in March 2020 at Abu Dhabi University when Covid-19 first wave hit. It was the best year, and I was very excited to join the first class. In this year, I created remarkable memories with my colleagues and my friends. I met great colleagues and friends that added sweetness to my journey. They are the reason I drove to success and received best knowledge. I also met the great professor and had a great talk with them. Confident I will keep in touch with them to share knowledge and thoughts.

In March 2021 while I did lots of research which university would be best for my coming journey as April 2021, I will put my application for the Ph.D. program. I'm thought of using my Ph.D. for teaching and administration. Searching and looking for a solid university that could support my dream is quite a journey itself. It took me months to gather and understand the entire process including searching, gathering the documents, applying for tests, and attending interviews that were needed for registration. Finally, in July, I got accepted into three universities, one in UAE and two abroad. After seeking an expert (former professor) and rendering the best knowledge and a distinguished reputation, I made my decision, and my first class was on 2 September 2021.

I'm aware that the whole process and the study won't be straightforward; nevertheless, I will put all my effort into accomplice it. You can plan for the long term but things change. I do have a plan; however, we don't know after 4-5 years what could happen. Things might change upon market demand. The message and the main point here is **keep going and chase your dream. If others and I can do it, then you can do it.**

Simultaneously, I'm trying to put my resume for a higher position in the same company; remember that with improving your qualifications, you need to move forward in your career life to build your resume in both sides. Also, remember not to stress yourself. Do your best, act, move, and recognize where it takes you. While my book is going through the publication process in March 2023, I am almost halfway through my Ph.D. journey and sincerely wish everyone their dream come true.

By reaching the end of second section, I wish you got the examples and ideas in how, what to do to make your journey smoother and enjoyable. Hoping by sharing my journey that could motive others and remind them that you're not alone. I wish when you finish reading my book that I motivated you to complete your education because this is my main purpose. With that being said, I wish the best luck to everyone in your own journey.

"Travel, in the younger sort, is a part of education; in the elder, a part of experience."

– Francis Bacon

Summary of Advice

I listed below the summary of advice I used in my book. This advice you may use it to follow and achieve your dream.

- Ask a lot to find the answer.
- Try various directions.
- Reach expert and discuss your problems or barriers.
- Share your issue with your beloved one.
- Create a new path that works for you.
- Use your strengths (empower your skills) and improve your weakness.
- Use different strategies to reach your goal.
- Be specific; reward yourself for small steps you took and the achievement you accomplished.
- Everything you wanted is one step outside your comfort zone.
- Finally, it's okay to feel down, express it, let out, and take a little break to breathe.

Delighted to hear your story:

If you reach the end, that means you're such an incredible person looking for success and an opportunity to learn. I wish you all the best. Thank you for reading my book; hope you enjoy it, and it benefits you. I will be delighted to hear your opinion, also, as I mentioned at beginning of my book, share any stories ideas that came to your mind with me, please don't hesitate to contact me at joreyalreyami@gmail.com.

Thank you ♡

Bibliography

M.Annie, Education vs. Experience: Which One Gets the Job? Investopedia, 2020

Ramdass D, Zimmerman BJ. Developing self-regulation skills: The important role of homework. Journal of advanced academics. 2011

Baumeister RF, Vohs KD, Oettingen G. Pragmatic prospection: How and why people think about the future. Review of General Psychology. 2016 Mar.

De Leo J. Quality education for sustainable development. UNESCO APNIEVE Australia; 2012.

Al Obaidli HY, Iqbal A. Digital forensics education in UAE. In2011 International Conference for Internet Technology and Secured Transactions 2011 Dec 11 (pp. 766–770). IEEE.

GHD Written by Jaime Herndon, Medically reviewed by Dr. Alana Biggers, Updated on 31 March 2017
www.healthline.com/health/turner-syndrome
Career development center, Qualifications or experience: what's more important?, totaljobs, 3 February 2020

www.totaljobs.com/advice/qualifications-or-experience-whats-more-important

Adebayo, F. A. (2015). Time management and students' academic performance in higher institutions, Nigeria a case study of ekiti state. *International Research in Education*, *3*(2), 1–12.

Strange, H. and Gibson, H. (2017). An investigation of experiential and transformative learning in study abroad programs. The Interdisciplinary Journal of Study Abroad, 29(1), pp. 85–100

Dewey, J. (1933). How we think, a restatement of the relation of the reflective thinking to the educative process. Boston, MA: Heath

Singelton, J. (2015). Head, heart, and hands model for transformative learning: Place as context for changing sustainability values. Journal of Sustainability Education. Available: http://www.jsedimensions.org/wordpress/content/2015/03/. [Accessed 17 January 2021].

Orr, D. (1992). Ecological literacy: Education and the Transition to a Postmodern World. Albany: NY: State University of New York.

Borup, J., Graham, C., West, R., Archambault, L., and Spring, K. Academic Communities of Engagement: an expansive lens for examining support structures in blended and online learning. Educational Technology Research and Development, 68(2), pp. 807–832.

Czerkawski, B. and Lyman, E. (2016). An Instructional Design Framework for Fostering Student Engagement in Online Learning Environments. TechTrends, 60(6), pp. 532–539.

Allen, J., Cars, G., and Madanipour, A. (2012). Social exclusion in European cities: processes, experiences, and responses. Routledge.

Bernt, M., and Colini, L. (2013). Exclusion, marginalization and peripheralization: Conceptual concerns in the study of urban inequalities (No. 49). Working paper.

Corrigan, P. W., and Shapiro, J. R. (2010). Measuring the impact of programs that challenge the public stigma of mental illness. Clinical psychology review, 30(8), 907–922.

Crow, L. (2010). Including all of our lives: Renewing the social model of disability. In Equality, Participation and Inclusion 1 (pp. 136–152). Routledge.

Devandas Aguilar, C. (2017). Social protection and persons with disabilities. International social security review, 70(4), 45–65.

Halmari, H. (2011). Political correctness, euphemism, and language change: The case of 'people first.' Journal of Pragmatics, 43(3), 828–840.

Jonassen, D. H., and Grabowski, B. L. (2012). Handbook of individual differences, learning, and instruction. Routledge.

Mintz, J., and Aagaard, M. (2012). The application of persuasive technology to educational settings. Educational Technology Research and Development, 60(3), 483–499.

Munyi, C. W. (2012). Past and present perceptions toward disability: A historical perspective. Disability studies quarterly, 32(2).

Nario-Redmond, M. R. (2019). Ableism: The causes and consequences of disability prejudice. John Wiley & Sons.

Oliver, M. (2018). A sociology of disability or a disablist sociology? In Disability and society (pp. 18–42). Routledge.

Patel, D. R., and Brown, K. A. (2017). An overview of the conceptual framework and definitions of disability. International Journal of Child Health and Human Development, 10(3), 247–252.

Pazey, B. L., and Cole, H. A. (2013). The role of special education training in the development of socially just leaders: Building an equity consciousness in educational leadership programs.

Educational Administration Quarterly, 49(2), 243–271.

Schur, L., Kruse, D., and Blanck, P. (2013). People with disabilities: sidelined or mainstreamed? Cambridge University Press.

Subotnik, R. F., Olszewski-Kubilius, P., and Worrell, F. C. (2011). Rethinking giftedness and gifted education: A proposed direction forward based on psychological science. Psychological science in the public interest, 12(1), 3–54.

Tranter, D. (2012). Unequal schooling: how the school curriculum keeps students from low socio-economic backgrounds out of university. International Journal of Inclusive Education, 16(9), 901–916.

Whyte, S. R., and Ingstad, B. (2020). 1. Disability and Culture: An Overview. Disability and culture, 1–32.

World Health Organization. (2019). Mental health, disability and human rights: WHO Quality Rights core training-for all services and all people: course guide.